# Letters of Love

Nadège René

# Letters of Love

For my mother Jacqueline René, please fly with this book to the heavens. For my dear brother Luca René, may you live a life more beautiful than our mother could have ever imagined.

For you.

# Foreword

*'The pull and reach of the invisible umbilical cord that drives the heart.'*

This line is taken from one of the pieces written for *Letters of Love.*
These words encapsulate so sweetly the essence of how *Letters of Love*
was conceived; and they are aligned, so intimately with the intentions of
the project on which this book rests. Although I am yet to feel the ecstasy
of having a child, I have felt what is described here; and this pull, for the
last seven and a half years, has guided pretty much everything that I do.

In January this year I attended a 'What If?' personal development
weekend in a crypt named Inspire, which lurks beneath an old church in
Elephant and Castle. I had no expectations of the course, and I knew very
little about it, I just went. That weekend, I saw young people who never
knew each other share the stories of their lives. Stories laced with fear
and grief, while everyone in the room listened, as we softened into a
space of alchemy. Since beginning this course in January, I have seen
transformation occur in every area of my life. I faced the prospect of
homelessness in July; I had a home in September. I repaired relationships
that had been falling apart. I finished a degree I had been grappling with
for four years and I performed in a professional theatre production that
honors the stories of young people who have left the care system.

*Letters of Love* is the foster child of the third What If Academy course,
'What If I Wrote a Book?' and upon first hearing of it; I became
passionately drawn to it. I have for as long as I can remember, been
enchanted by words, and I am mesmerized by creative expression. I
believe that the two combine gorgeously. Nonetheless, a series of lines
that read beautifully on a page is not what we are concerned with. Here,
we are playing a much, much bigger game...

There are five of us on this course, and the books serve as an expression
of the thing we each love in the world. But since beginning this course,
the book has become so much more, it has given me a new context by
which to view my life. The world of personal development has had me
exploring some of the darkest corners of who I am, and pouring love into
those cracks, stenciling me toward the purpose of the book. Although I
did not see it, by late October, the 'thing' that my book would be based
on was glowing... love.

Love is the thing that I crave in every scenario, and it has been the bottom line (whether I've realized it or not) of all the work I have done. Despite there being very little on this earth that is of greater value to me, it is the thing that I resist and fear the most. I have experienced an indescribable amount of pain in my life and love has always beckoned me further towards it, and now I can be of greater service because of it. Love led me to the hostels, to the men, to the financial and living circumstances that devoured me. Little did I know, love was training me. Love taught me the humility and value of being of service to other people, showing me how people can help to heal other people. Love tore from me like flesh everything I ever held dear, so that I could appreciate and go about life in a particular kind of way. Love has led me to all the magnificent things and people that I now have in my life. It led me here, writing this, right now.

On Saturday 7th November 2015, I began to make requests of people to contribute to *Letters of Love*. Every single letter that was sent to me has gone into the book. There is no process of elimination. Having read the manuscript in its entirety, I believe many of the letters come from the same place as the quote I included in the beginning of this foreword. Whether I like the letters or not, so long as a letter adheres to the guidelines I set out when making a request, it is not at all my business to remove it. The purpose of this book is not about reaching a particular level of literary excellence, or even punctuation or grammar. The magic is in the honesty of the expression. Authentic expression particularly is a thing that I know many feel starved of in this world. I have learnt so much about love, ego, judgement and acceptance through this process.

*'The pull and reach of the invisible umbilical cord that drives the heart'*

Is a line in in the book that conveys the feeling that has been the genesis of *Letters of Love,* and this theme permeates through all the letters that make up this book. The idea that one line, or even one word, from a book woven together by the generous and courageous sharing of 46 individuals can reach a person in a way that could change their mind about the world. The book provides the opportunity for all 46 contributing authors to have an expression of *their* love in the world, and I am so honored to have been the clearing for that.

# The What If Academy

The What If Academy is a young people's not for profit transformative training organization. It believes that young people have an infinite potential and capacity to transform their lives and the world around them. The What If Academy knows that every young person can make positive choices for themselves given the correct training, tools, guidance and community. Ultimately these positive choices will empower, enable and encourage young people to make healthy, safe, positive decisions which will benefit not only themselves and their immediate circle but society as a whole.

The What If Academy delivers the type of commercially expensive personal development programmes to 18-30 year olds for free that are available for individuals to purchase for thousands of pounds. Young people do not typically consider financially investing in their own development after participating in traditional, informative education for many years. Once informative education finishes, many young adults find themselves in a large amount of debt and feelings of struggle and incompleteness as they enter the world of independent adulthood and all the expectations that world brings.

The What If Academy delivers training to young people that focus on difficult areas of their lives. We do not shy away from the difficult issues or situations young people bring. We embrace these difficulties as the first step to moving towards a positive future. It isn't magic but rather experiential learning processes that are taught during our unique three-day training course, The What If Weekend, and in the other courses that follow. We also offer individual and bespoke transformative training and work with professionals and in systems in our society that simply do not work, and in many cases, make life worse for those who they touch.

What If?... Young people understood themselves and why they make the choices they make?
What If?... Young people recognised that they were the masters of their universe?
What If?... Young people believed in themselves?
What If?... Young people were able to learn that anything was possible?
What If?... Young people communicated in a way that maximised engagement and understanding?
What If?... Young people created a world that worked for everyone?

The What If Academy programmes address these questions and transform the limiting beliefs young people hold about themselves. It allows them to step into a future where their hopes, dreams and ambitions can be realised. We do not make this statement lightly and we confidently state that all of these outcomes are possible through their participation in our programmes.

### What If I Wrote a Book?

What If I Wrote a Book is a 12-week programme that What If Academy Graduates can apply for once they have completed the What If Weekend, a minimum of eight What If Evening sessions and What If We Cared?. This is the final programme in our year-long transformative curriculum.

What If I Wrote a Book? allows young people to discover what they truly love in life and to use that knowledge to create a book that they produce and publish culminating in a group book launch. Each book comprises of a collection of letters written by people the participants of the programme make requests of. This programme trains participants to make powerful requests of others and to hold themselves and others accountable for the agreements they make. Participants learn how to respond to let downs, to broken promises, and explore their own relationship to keeping their word. This book project must be completed within the specific time duration of the course to ensure that each book is available for purchase at the time of the book launch. Essentially, What If I Wrote a Book? is about training participants in authentic creative leadership skills, transformative project management approaches; and these skills are transferrable to all areas of their lives.

Specific outcomes:
- Young people explore for themselves and identify within a group setting what they love and what they are authentically passionate about in life
- Participants select a topic for their book based on their understanding of what they authentically love
- They are trained in how to make requests of others to contribute the content of their book
- They are trained in how to manage their feelings and reactions in relation to the process of creating the book. It builds their confidence, self-esteem and leadership skills
- They collaboratively organise a book launch
- They learn the process of how to self-publish a book
- They are trained in how to speak powerfully in public
- They learn the impact of altruistic contribution to others who may read the book as a source of inspiration, connection and hope
- A book they have created from nothing exists in the world as an expression of their individual integrity and authenticity

To find out more about The What If Academy, and to find out how to support us, please visit our website:
www.whatifacademy.org.uk


**Why What If I Wrote a Book?**
**Sarah Parry**
**Founder and CEO**
**The What If Academy**

In December 2013 my friend Emma left a community organisation we both worked at. Emma had brought me to this organisation to help her run a parenting programme that supported the most vulnerable parents in South London. Emma had decided to move back to her beloved Hull in the North of England and I was going to miss her. I knew I needed to do something important to acknowledge her leaving and one morning I woke up and thought I'd put together a book for her. The book would be letters of acknowledgement of how Emma had impacted the lives of the people in the communities she served throughout her career spanning almost two decades.

I had heard that it was pretty straightforward to self-publish a book on Amazon and thought that most people only really get acknowledged when they die! I'm all about the living and so; 'Letters to Emma, How One Social Worker Changed the World' was born. My friend Sally Swingewood incidentally popped up on my Facebook feed at the precise moment I decided the book would happen and I eagerly told her my idea; she then told me that she'd just self-published a book on Amazon and she would do all the online self-publishing stuff for me. Synchronicity in action! I love it when the universe does that.

I spent the next three weeks asking every person who knew Emma to write a letter to her for the book. The staff and community members at the organisation where we both worked all rallied around and wrote their letters with love and diligence. They saw it as an opportunity to express gratitude and love and willingly and graciously emailed me letter after letter for Emma. That experience taught me a lot about community and later contributed to how I structured the What If programmes. Next, the harder stuff; an organisation where Emma and I worked for many years where we met, and where she helped hundreds and hundreds of children; no one wrote a single letter to her. Not a single person submitted a letter for her. Not one. Nada. Nothing. Zip. Zero. You get the picture? I negotiated, emailed, called, and still nothing. I now know that this was about the lack of leadership within the organisation and no one championed the writing of these letters for Emma. There was lots of fear and suspicion and this toxic position was led by the Director of Children's Services there. She held the position that it was too grand an acknowledgement of one person, and rather all success is a team effort. It's my view that every single team member should be grandly acknowledged for helping another human. Her position taught me a lot about leadership and how easy it is for us to use our power to diminish another's light. I had quite a few resentments after that conversation I can tell you!

I had endless conversations with my dear friend Colleen while in the process of requesting these letters. I would call her angry, frustrated, inspired, moved, outraged, humbled – and mostly in tears. Colleen would regularly ask me, "Sarah, were you clear in your request?" Me, "Yes but why haven't they sent their letter yet?!", Colleen, "Sarah, you have to leave them to get back to you or not, it's up to them now". Me, "Ugh!" [cue catalogue of grumpy, frustrated noises!] Colleen was my supporter, coach and compassionate friend throughout the process and I am forever grateful to her for that. Colleen now heads up The What If Academy's Board and we experience her leadership, her compassion and her energy in all areas of our work.

The creation of this book taught me so much. I discovered how much courage it takes to be vulnerable enough to make a request from another human being when you really want the answer to be a yes. I realised that all creations need support, and they need love. I found out that I really am quite unstoppable when I really believe in something. I saw what can be achieved when community comes together. I saw how nothing can be created when leadership isn't present. I learnt that deadlines are opportunities to perform. I learnt that I loved Emma so much more than I ever thought I did. And once the book was published and as Emma's dad read the Forward he had written to surprise her at her leaving do, I realised the community saw me as a different kind of leader; in their eyes I represented something new and it was all very good.

There are so many people to thank for the creation of the book you are about to read.
Emma Vine for being a social worker who relentlessly and professionally loved children and inspired all of this. All of the Letters to Emma letter writers for their generosity and love. The community in and around the organisation Emma and I worked at **www.in-spire.org.uk** for their compassion, understanding and love. Colleen Humphrey for sticking with me and sticking with the amazingness of the book. Susann Ribeck for teaching me what it takes to lead with authenticity and a lot of love. Sally Swingewood for her support, practical help (all leaders need help!) and for giving us Freya. Fiona for all the proof reading and for being excited for me when the book arrived! Michelle Cohen and Catherine Lomas who listened to many a whinge! Thank you so much.

This book is one of the most challenging projects I have ever undertaken (and I've set up and managed many projects in my time) It wasn't until 18 months after the book was published that I wrote What If I Wrote a Book? as a transformative training programme for young people.

What If I Wrote a Book? was born out of Letters to Emma. The book you are about to read, while distinct in its title, is really all about leadership and commitment.

As you read the letters, please think about what it took for the creator of the book to put it together. Please consider that it required them to be powerful and vulnerable at the same time, no easy task. Please consider that the skills required to create this book are exactly the same skills that are required to create world peace.

The book you are about to read is written by a courageous, loving, committed young adult who believes that the world can be created to work for everyone; and they now know how to do it.

Much love,
Sarah x

*'Forget logic,*
*Forget your head.*
*Open your heart,*
*and come*
*with me.'*

*-Marianne Williamson*

# Letters of Love

Inappropriate inside jokes.

#  الـحـب

What is love………
Truth and Honesty.
It's getting on the dance floor knowing full well you have no business being there but that's the level of courage she gives you.
It's growth.
It's when you're sitting on the tube and your eyes meet on the window reflection.
It's being on your phone knowing it's time to delete those pics you took together and that message thread but you put it off not knowing that you'll be ok and you'll make new memories.
It's when she comes home from the library late and you make sure she has something to eat before bed, fueling that degree mentally and physically.
It's inappropriate inside jokes.
It's that walk after dinner at that restaurant when you're arm in arm or hand in hand and no words are spoken or needed, just the sound of each other's footsteps.
Its comfortable silences.
It's the pain of waking up one day and you don't speak the same language anymore.
It's freshly made home cooked meals and sitting together to watch fresh prince of bel air.
It's separate but equal.
It's being at the gym or on the bus remembering that night and how good it was, having that involuntary smile.
It's not being able to admit certain realities to yourself.
It's when you notice her nuances and quirks and you smile to yourself when they occur.
It's loving her the way she is and then helping her be what she wants to be.
It's when your chest feels like it's in a vice because you want them and miss them so bad but they don't have a clue and even if they did you're not sure they'd understand.
It's seeing beauty without a mirror or compliments.
It's hearing that song that boosts dopamine & serotonin levels.
It's loving yourself, it's letting yourself be loved, and it's not setting yourself on fire to keep others warm.
-Michael Gichia

My love.
Your love.
His love.
Her love.

# HOW IS LOVE

I wonder how Eros is doing today,
Does he still lay in wait, ready to prey?
On weary travelers hungry for affection, cold and lonely in need of
protection.
Or in this age has his kill been forgotten.
Supplanted and replaced by the click of a button.
Where all one has to do is type, sit back and ponder then wait for a bite.
His older siblings Philia and Storge are much employed in this modern
day.
Hard to buy your family online, and love for mankind was never blind.
But they I fear may too be redacted.
By movements and laws recently enacted.
That calls into question the very nature of love.
My love, your love, his love, her love.
For humanity in love to continue to charm.
It seems to me we must do no harm.
For the pure and true mystery that comes from above.
Is that we are the very embodiment of love.

*-Jason Morgan*

Love will set you free.

Dear Mum,

I know that a huge reason that I am okay today is that I always knew that you loved me. I never questioned it growing up. It didn't have to look the same as everyone else's parent-child relationship. No one could tell me otherwise.

I always knew you didn't love yourself though. On my weekend visits I watched you work hard; driving the buses, in the circus, the slaughterhouse, in the gardens and the nurseries, and at the flower shows. You were never without work. You never had much money, yet you always had food in the fridge, fuel in the tank and wood on the fire. To others, you seemed content.

But I saw the quiet moments. I heard how you talked about yourself. I saw your face as you explained to your friends and strangers when they asked where your kids were. You always 'came clean' about us being in foster care, as though their judgement of you as an imperfect mother was your rightful punishment.

I watched you retreat and numb yourself with drugs. It made me sad to see that, but I tried never to judge you poorly because of it. I hated those visits to your dealer. The smoke in that dingy flat was so thick and I don't think you knew I had asthma. It seemed to enable you to have just a little peace though.

I obviously met the boyfriend's you chose. I do not want to absolve their responsibility in any way, but perhaps you allowed them to treat you the way you truly felt about yourself. I saw the wrestle inside of you as you grieved the loss of your children and the death of Dad, your true love. I think you tolerated the violence from those men because you thought you deserved it. I think you fought with the fear of being alone too.

When you were single, I saw the word 'solo' written in capitals on the walls of your caravan in green highlighter pen. Even then I knew it was written out of anger and despair. It wasn't a declaration for us kids to take personally.

I learned to read your behavior and I knew it wasn't about us kids. I learned to love you with forgiveness. Not because I am a martyr or some higher being, but because I knew that without forgiveness you held yourself captive.

I have often thought that it's easier to give love than to receive love. But, I am trying to learn that love flows in one direction – in fact, I think it's something you always give...

I am learning to give love to myself as I grow to know myself, and I feel that forgiveness is enveloped within that. There's nothing more vulnerable than forgiveness though, but it's better to hurt through healing, than to just hurt, for hurting's sake. It's time you forgave yourself Mum. Not because us kids say so though, because it's the only way to set yourself free. *-Number 3*

Come dance in the rain with me.

Would I be the man that I am if you didn't happen?
Would I even be where I stand if you didn't happen!
In a world full of pain you're my sun in the rain
You give me motivation to get up and go again.
It's just us against the earth... the odds are low, but I got a good feeling!
Can't really explain love...
But if I look in your eyes then I get the meaning
I find them healing
My tranquility in a fucked up world that ain't meant for me
Caught in the storm, but we're here now so let's make the most of it...

Come dance in the rain with me
Close your eyes and let's dream of a place where we don't have to
struggle to stay alive
Even though I can't lie, I find a pleasure in the hustle... If it means you
survive!
I'll put it all on the line if it means you will thrive.
I'll gladly leave my belly to rumble as long as you've been fed
You gave us a home, in a house with nothing but an old fridge and a bed
And it might all be in my head...
But you make this council flat feel like a mansion instead
I'll gladly sleep on the floor... but I know you'll make space in da bed!
What's mine is yours before I even get it
Let's be honest...
I may never even get it...
But I'm cool as long as you got it!
It's a simple as that... I put else nothing above
And I hold warmth in my heart knowing love is love!

*-Jemal Peters*

Heroine.

Dear Brother,

     She makes me so jealous, that heroin of yours. I tried to love, but love had too many side effects for you; it left your skin too tender to be poked at with needles. I never gave you that ultimatum, but still you chose her.

     A xx

Loving you has consumed me.

17.11.15

A letter to my son…
You will never know the depth of my love for you and why should you?
A mother will always tell her children how much she loves them and find
a million ways to show them, but she will never be able to convey the
agony and ecstasy of loving; the pull and reach of the invisible umbilical
cord that drives the heart.

Children say they only understand a parent's love once they have children
of their own. When you have children, and I pray you do, you will have a
better perspective, but right now, let me try to put the unspoken into
words.

Loving you has consumed me. I have never separated my heart from your
soul; for every heart wrenching pain you have ever felt, I have grieved; a
ripping of my heart. Every time you have been misunderstood or wronged
by others, I have leapt to your defence and tried to smother the hurt.
Every time your anger has boiled to a dangerous level of uprising, I have
been paralysed by fear for your liberty; the life of a young, black man is
perilously fearsome, a minefield. Every time your anger has dissolved
into tears I have wanted to cradle you like I could when you were my
baby. Defensively proud, you have not let me near. On the nights, when I
know you are sleeping safely in your bed, I have thanked God for the
feeling of overwhelming peace. The happy days have filled me with a
deep, bubbling joy, diffusing the pain, inspiring hope, fuelling your
future.
And I need you to have a future, a satisfying future, a future fit for a man
who has passed through a coming of age threshold of pain and become a
profoundly wise king among demons.

Your Mum, XX

Sex isn't love.

Love is kind
Love is unconditional
We were addicts and sex was our drug
We fucked through our problems
Until we realised that sex isn't love
Our validation was our body and without that we were nothing
So we drifted, sex non-existent
The spark was gone
Only to be reignited by his call
"Sorry babe, I'm going to change"
Then we're back to fucking like animals
Making promises we won't keep
Back to square 1
So now we playing happy families
Oscar performances
"We can make it work; I just need to be patient"
So I wait for that guy he promised me
He doesn't turn up
"I just don't think I'm ready" he says
But he already has my heart
My soul

*-Anonymous*

Love pours itself.

What is love?

What is love? I hear you ask. Love is your very own truth. It's what the loyalties of the soul is, the depths of your mind. It's what empowers others to fall for you & inspires the chapters to the ever writing life story. Love, lust and loss all go together in the spells that cast over this universe. Love can fall into a million pieces and still smash right through the heart, tying promises with ribbons made of glue. Love is a powerful collusion between heart & mind. The soul is the middle man. There's no logic to love... it's free flowing. We all get it, we all want it, we all give it. Self-love is the core; self-love is the empress to the kingdoms of home truths. Authentic in its feeling, delusional in its appearance. We do many things for love but most people give up on it. Stay true & it'll stay true to you. For love is your very own truth... There are no limits on how much love can grow. The rain can fall forever, puddles splash dreams so deeply embedded into the hearts of strangers, love meets you every day if you know what you're looking for.

Clink the glasses to cheers the future.

Pasts linger in the red wine bottles.

Love pours itself.

-*Shannen L. Gilbert*

She always remembers.

# But It's Love…Isn't It?

His phone rings. Her heart beat quickens,
That ring, that bloody ring.
He looks at the screen - then looks away,
They both know, who it is.
They share a laugh and for a moment she forgets,
But laughter turns into sadness.
She remembers,
She always remembers.

Months pass by, isolation deepens,
Friends are *sick* of hearing, family have given up.
But that phone,
**Won't**. **Stop**. **Ringing**.

False promises, deceit and lies.
The glow she once had – gone,
This is what love is though, isn't it?
Commitment?
His phone rings. Her heart beat steady.
That ring, so melancholy, so free.
'It's over' she declares voice shaking,
**It's over. It's over. It's over.**

Baby girl 7lb 5. oz

# Love letters in a digital age
By Robin Clisby

<Text Messages        **Mom**        Details

Me: Mom, I tried to call you a few times, but I keep missing you. Don't want you to find out via social media. Congratulations! You are finally going to be a grandma! Call me!

Mom: I am so happy I am doing a little dance! How many weeks?

Me: 7. Apparently, it is the size of an olive.

Mom: Are you taking vitamins?

Me: Yes

Mom: Which ones? Do they have folic acid and calcium?

Me: Yes, they have folic acid and calcium.

Mom: Oh good, as long as you are taking vitamins.

Mom: How are you feeling honey?

Me: Terrible. I think the baby is trying to kill me.

Mom: That's normal. Drink ginger tea and eat crackers.

Me: I tried, but the smell of ginger makes me nauseous. Why didn't you tell me it was going to be like this?

Mom: Because someday I wanted to be a grandma:) Sorry you don't feel well honey. Just remember, morning sickness is meant to be a sign everything is going well.

Me: I'll try to remember that next time I'm throwing up.

Mom: You feeling any better?

Me: Not really :(

Me: We had our 12 week scan today! It was amazing. You could see the baby's spine and heart!

Mom: Way cool! Everything look okay?

Me: Yeah, the doctor said everything looked good.

Mom: Little boy or girl?

Me: Too early to tell.

Mom: Whatever it is, it will be perfect! I can't believe I am going to be a grandmother! Hurray!

Me: :) it is exciting! I hope the baby likes me.

Mom: Of course it will like you. All babies love their mothers, until they become teenagers!

Me: Oh good. Something else to look forward too. :(

Me: Mom, I am sorry I was such a crappy teenager. I am really, really lucky to have you.

Mom: Don't worry about it honey. We are all crappy teenagers. Love to you, hubby and bump.

Mom: You still getting the bad morning sickness?

Me: I feel creepily good. Being sick got to be weirdly comforting. At least I knew the baby was still in there.

Mom: Don't worry. The baby is still in there.

Me: The baby was facing the wrong way so we couldn't see the sex. Guess we will be having a surprise.

Mom: I love surprises!

Mom: Have you seen these Granny pod things? If I lived in your backyard, I could babysit all the time.

Me: Ahh. Something to think about. I don't think our garden is big enough :(

Me: According to the baby app,the baby is now the size of a watermelon.

Me: Nursery finished! Thanks for the rocking chair! I absolutely love it.

Mom: Do you want me to fly over for the birth?

Me: yes please!

Mom: Okay, I will be there.

Mom: You are not having a home birth are you? Your grandmother said you were thinking of having a home birth. I think it is a bad idea. Anything could happen.

Me: Don't worry mom. I'm only thinking about it.

Me: It's time!

Mom: I'm on my way to the airport! You're gong to the hospital right?

Me: False Alarm. Braxton Hicks. :(

Mom: I'm still coming. Don't worry about picking me up. I'll get a cab.

Me: When do you land? Will send J to come get you. A taxi will cost you a fortune.

Me: Soo, it was a false, false alarm. We are on are way to the hospital. J will keep you posted.

Me: Hey Grandma lady, its your favourite son in law, Mum and baby doing fine. Baby girl 7lb 5. oz.

Mom: I am so happy! Almost there. I can't wait to hold my babies in my arms. Love to you all and see you soon!

Love is silent.

My dear Love,

Love how are we keeping today? May I know what...

Love is when you are able to look your partner in the eye and ignore their bad breath and proceed to give them a heartfelt endearing KISS....

Love is silent, Love is loud, Love is blind, Love is bold. Love is an emotion is it…..

Grand finale of LOVE when your heart skips a beat when you look lovely at your chosen object and admit you are in love!!!!!!

Yours sincerely,
Janice René

Deep and potent oceans.

Dear love,

You're deceptive,

Elusive,

Unnecessary.

At least that's what I've been told when I declare my dedication of
learning to swim your deep and potent oceans.
I once believed I wasn't meant to experience you. It seemed like every
moment I came to your shores, the water just a tad too cold, or the day
was too hot to leave my home. But I've come to understand, that the
folklore behind resistance was just that: stories. Stories of scared souls
afraid to swim because the water's too deep, too mysterious, for them to
try again.
I'm sorry. You were just a pure spirit that we've mislabelled once we
added saturations to your essence.
I just wanted to say thank you, for letting me live.

*-Dae.*

Sweet and feisty like sugar cane.

I call him Caine
He don't like that, I don't care, that's his name
He teaches me I'm beautiful, empowers me worthy of inspirational
This surge that's become an urge strikes like sharp shocks it's unusual
We're sweet & feisty like sugar cane
Well not exactly, more like euphoria mixed with bitter pain
But he's so sexy as I watch him strut to Hip hop
As the creases and knots of his cool frown forms across caramel skin
Aesop's Daylight dawns and I swear he's got the birds to sing
I know I can't get too attached, I already know I can't fuck with him like
that
Until he asks me to taste... Well he's my best friend so go–start
But don't lose the fight to your heart
But I'm losing; he makes me breathless and pant
How a sistah would feel after fuckin' with the coco plant

I call him Caine
He don't like that, I don't care, that's his name
Still breathless I got my first hit, God, now I want more
Addicted to his soul and already closer to the bedroom door
I wrap my arms around his neck, seal my body to his chest
Finally surrendering, accepting that after this he's mine for sure
And he is as we slide off the mattress, tongue-embraced, hitting the
bedroom floor
While in heaven we ignite the war of Armageddon, franchise the rush of
Paradise
Then he cracks... and I break in half like a twig that's snapped
The moment is raw because I'm high sitting in ecstasy's lap–in Caine's
lap
Apart from God, only the man who I become one with can see me
vulnerable like that
I am in love, and from its infancy
It's been a year of conversational intimacy wondering once he touched
me
How it would feel when he controlled the blood flow in my veins

I call him Crack Cocaine
He don't like that, I don't care, that's his name
I'm fighting my addiction, jonesing a heartache knowing I can't have him
He told me it wouldn't last but I fought another battle hoping that didn't
pass
'Til reality and his no longer wanting me, tore him from my hands
I warranted my pillows end; soaked and drowned 'em
Yet our emotional instability leaves us sending each other our poems

To read them, though, a tease straight from hell; 'There are 8 wonders in the world
And you would be the 9th…if you want to be my girl'
I fight those hopeless fantasies of his arms around me,
As another line reads 'poems that remind you of me when you get lonely'
Drives me crazy then I get angry
With the idiotic questions he asks me, as if he just met me
Don't stare at me with your euphoric glow and ask me if we can be friends
Don't ask me now, don't ask me out loud, just sit with me, act like you said, act like I heard
I'm tender, needing to recover and accept not ever being able to share his last name; BeFree
Yes, now that's his name, he likes that name
But until I can be free of his being, I call him Caine.

-Tox Mahogany

I suppose it's an unwritten obligation.

To whom this may concern,

This may come as a surprise to you, but I was given something to hold for you, I've been looking after it for a while now. I suppose it's an unwritten obligation for being your neighbour. I take it with me when I leave the house, just in case burglars break in.

I thought I lost it on a train once, even felt to lose it on purpose if I'm honest, I haven't seen you since I signed for it. Do you not check your mail, I'm sure the postman left you a note to say I have it. Maybe you overlooked it.

Perhaps I should give it to someone who'll look after it better than me, I never asked for this responsibility. What time do you finish work, I never see you coming home, I've been by my window waiting.

I want you a reward, it's only right. As much as I have tried to pawn off something that doesn't belong to me, to people who tell me and show me it's worthless. But this is yours, and I will keep it safe until you come home from whatever it is that has your attention.

Next time, you ask for something to be delivered to you, make sure you're in when opportunity knocks. I'm not as patient as I should be. If you don't hurry up and get what's yours, I'll give it to whoever knocks next.

Warmest Regards
LionHeart

We laugh until we're in tears.

To my family of friends,

It is hard to find the right words to express exactly how much I love my friends. And even if I could I don't think I could squeeze it all into one page, if you take into consideration the 7 years' worth of friendship, 84 months of happiness, 2,555 days spent making memories, 61,320 hours of laughter, 3679200 minutes of caring and every second spent establishing true friendship. True friends are hard to find but I'm lucky enough to have found five amazing friends. My friends are more than just friends they are family and I love my small extended family of five. This is a letter of love to the five girls that mean the world to me.

I love that I am able to be myself when I'm around you all and not feel uncomfortable or judged. I love that whenever we meet up we laugh until we're in tears (mainly me). I love that there's never any fighting between us. I love that we're all supportive of each other's goals and ambitions. I love that we inspire each other. I love that we can be honest. But most importantly I love that you walked into my life at the right time and stuck by my side.

Even to those old friends who I have spent a lifetime with I love you. And new friends who I will embark on a brand new journey with me I love you as well.

There is no such thing as a perfect recipe for friendship but if there was it would look a little like this:

1 Pint of Clarissa for Laughter

75g of Joyce for Craziness

A Teaspoon of Teresa for Sincerity

3 Cups of Thamirys for a Bag of fun

2 Spoonfuls of Georgia for Kindness

200g of Justyne for Understanding

¼ Cup of K-ci for Thoughtfulness

A Pinch of Hannah for Loyalty

And a Sprinkle of Jennifer for Sweetness

Blend together with a handful Love and spread over a life time.

Thank you for all being a part of my life!

Lots of Love

Leah xxx

.

You are my home.

### "Love is Home" By J Nuclear

*Love... makes me follow you into the darkness as you glow,
I've memorized the movements from the lights of your soul,
you are better than I've ever dreamed something that I've
never known....you are my home*

*I would lift the weight of the whole world for a thousand
years if it would grant me just one moment to hold you, to
touch you, to love you as I become you, I would snatch life
from the jaws of death, if it meant I could save you and spare
your last breath, I would swim across an ocean of fire, if on
the other side I could reach your love I require, I would walk
a million miles across burning sands, if it would take me to
the embrace of your nurturing hands, because you are better
than I've ever dreamed something that I've never known...
you are my home*

*I can hear your heart beat from far away... it matches the
rhythm of mine, whenever you're close the spiritual
connection is divine, oh how near is the day that you shall
only be mine, I can see you in the distance, like a star... but
you eclipse it, your beauty is so exquisite, I struggle with your
existence, because you are better than I've ever dreamed,
something that I've ever known... you are my home.*

# A
# rebellious,
# teenage red

That's not. No. I'm sitting on my bed. Near the wall we painted together. A rebellious, teenage red, with some new chips in it. And. Love? Do I love her in this moment? She sits with me. Still, with staccato edges. Angular elbows, fingers locked. We both look up, and that's not it, no.

Before, it started with a noise. The camera turning on. I knew it from our holidays, but never expected to need to remember it. That noise goes with a smiling face somewhere. Sand, strewn in sun-warmed hillocks against a wavering blue. That noise becomes a book of photos. An expression of love.

But not then. Me alone. Naked, out of the shower, in front of the glass. My mirror body fading slowly into steam. It was a punctuation mark on a soft silence, the noise, that noise. A camera. Where? Up.

There's a shout. Mine. A hand slides a bolt. Mine. Silence. Ours.

And his footsteps in the attic are purposeful, moving away. The camera has gone from my ceiling. Just a hole, now. Stay in my room. Phone numbers? Never expected to need to remember them. No. Quiet. Just be quiet.

She came back from the funeral two days later and we had guests. Chatting, they need tea. Kitchen. Me and her alone for a second, I said, "Mum, did he mention?" "Anything about a camera?"
I thought she'd panic, but she said
"No, let me ask him".
We went back in.

…

Somebody (him or her) said to do a re-enactment. Re-enact the scene that happened when mum was away. Replay the disputed night. Positions please. Lights, camera.  And now he is up there, my stepdad, putting a pipe through the hole in my ceiling. Maybe, behind the white plaster, up in the dark, he has his fingers crossed. Because, 'I was fixing a pipe', he said, to her.

That's not. No. I'm sitting on my bed. Near the wall we painted together. A rebellious, teenage red, with some new chips in it. And. Love? Do I love her in this moment? She sits with me. Still, with staccato edges. Angular elbows, fingers locked. We both look up, and that's not it, no. It's a pipe.

That is not the same as what I saw that night. Me alone. Naked, out of the shower, in front of the glass.

I start to shake my hea-

"Do you know what will happen?" She asked - and then told me in the same breath. I heard her say prison.

My sister? 'At risk' list. Poor Emma, no father to talk about at school. Is this a pipe I see before me?

Only a moment to decide.

I think about my (half) sister. More than half a sister to me.

I said, "Okay". Moment crashes, blue wave on yellow beach. I said "That is what I saw".

A peeping pipe.

We forgot all about the noise. The punctuation mark. The question that I looked up to answer.

We did it for Emma.

We did it for love.

The tyrant fighting the system.

I mostly only write poetry for you

otherwise my stanzas are based on

politics I know very little about.

I know enough to be angry

I want you to be my politics

you're the passion that fills my heart

I will be the tyrant fighting

the system

my fingers will write the riots

I would be your prisoner

sitting in solitary confinement

and suffering graciously

for the cause

tap my cell bars

with your tin cup

fall in love with my revolution


*- Pia Leiba*

You don't even know you're in it.

Love can be strange to those who don't understand it, some people mistake it for obsession some even resent it. Yes, you can be loved and not love and it also works the other way round, however love is most beautiful when there's a direct connection making it mutual. What makes love hard to understand is that there are different forms, the love you have for your mother is a different love you'll have for your lover. Love can be mysterious, sometimes you don't even know you're in it, your mind may be saying one thing whilst your feelings express something else, especially if it's your first time as it makes it harder to tell. The first time I fell in love I learnt something new straight away, falling in love at first sight is real whether you notice it right there and then or not. It's more than a "I think she's nice" it's a "I need to know who you are" and I'm lucky enough to say it was mutual. I found myself falling with no choice in the matter, it was natural not forced, not fake, uncontrollable. It felt like there was a new spring in my step maybe my smile was different and everyone noticed. Love is the freshest breath of air life has to offer and the best part about that breath is you get to share it, two beings one breath and that is what love is two people becoming one indulging in romance, companionship, joy, happiness and laughter despite the ups or downs. Can you fall out of love? Yes, this may make you question how authentic the experience was but you shouldn't question the authenticity because when you know, you know. If you can no longer recognise the person you fell in love with in your partner then you'll start to feel the change. Love is unconditional consistency that promotes growth, whilst an inconsistent love may lead to growth apart. These are all the things I've learnt with my first encounter finding love, a lesson I've cherished and have no regrets about, without a doubt an experience like no other.

"Spoil me with your consistency, remain the same you and you won't have to worry about a different me" -Wale.

This is my letter of love.

-Fabian Jones

I ran up and down every court after every loose ball for you.

# For the love of the game

Dear basketball,

From the moment I started rolling up my socks and shooting imaginary game-winning shots in the great western forum I knew one thing was real, I fell in love with you.

A love so deep I gave you my all,
From my mind and body, to my spirit and soul.
As a six year old boy deeply in love with you I never saw the end of the tunnel. I only saw myself running out of one, and so I ran.
I ran up and down every court after every loose ball for you.
You asked for my hustle, I gave you my heart because it came with so much more.

I played through the sweat and hurt,
Not because challenge called me, but because you called me.
I did everything for you because that's what you do when someone makes you feel as alive as you've made me feel.
You gave a six-year old boy his hoop dreams and I'll always love you for it.

But I can't love you obsessively for much longer.
This season is all I have left to give. My heart can take the pounding, my mind can handle the grind but my body knows it's time to say goodbye.
And that's OK.

I'm ready to let you go
I want you to know so we both can savor every moment we have left together.
The good and the bad. We have given each other all that we have.
And we both know, no matter what I do next I'll always be that kid with the rolled up socks, dust bin in the corner with the voice in my head
":05 seconds on the clock, ball in my hands.

5...4...3...2...1, SWISH"

When I say love you.

When I walked away from my ex, I never believed that I could possibly love another man again. However, now that I have met you I know it was not about if I would love another but instead it was if I wanted to. You have helped me to see the true meaning of love. You see I believed someone telling me they loved me was enough because why else would they speak the word love from their mouth. What would they possibly gain? I know now that the meaning of love for many is lost. It is thrown around so much nowadays that we think it's ok to use it for our own selfish gain, despite the hurt it may cause to another. When I say I love you it means I would do just about anything to be with you, even if it meant surrendering my life or giving up my happiness for yours. However, I realized when he said he loved me it was nothing but an invisible chain around my neck, holding me closer and weakening me every step of the way. You see he thought the long conversation on the phone; the periods of time spent together and/or the passion we shared beneath the covers were enough. However, his unwillingness to fight for our relationships, his lack of input, inability to take a chances and his own selfish pride let me know that he didn't truly love me. In fact I was just the toy in his life that was there for only one purpose and that was to fulfil his own happiness. And like many toys, once it has served its purpose it would be no longer valuable, which is why I had to go. However, through me going it led me straight to you. Some would call you a rebound, meaning that you too have only one purpose and that is for my own selfish happiness. Although I know with you that is not the case. I believe it was God that brought us together and for that I am truly grateful. You have blessed me in so many ways. You have lightened up both my heart and my mind. So today I would like to say I love you and I hope my love for you never dies. However, if it does please believe me when I said this to you, I meant it from the bottom of my heart.


Today I made the decision to love another and that is you.
Regards
Lisa

Why do I confuse being drunk
with being in love?

Dear Claire,
I understand you, when nobody else does. No day is the same for you, but it seems the rest carry on as normal. I know you've been hurt, but nobody else does, and if I do tell them they would never consider me for love. How do I overcome the issue with my past? How do I stop myself confusing lust with love? How can I trust someone who only wants a one night stand? One day I'm high on life and I know I could take on everything, however, the next I just seem to crash and see the doom in any love I may find or not. People are confused as to why one minute I'm positive about love, however, the next I am not. I make up stories in my head about what my perfect husband will look like, sound like, treat me like, and just know they will be holding my hand until the end of my time on this earth. Maybe I trust men too much? Maybe I trust them with the wrong things? Maybe I should never have kissed him so soon, maybe I shouldn't have told him about my life story, or am I in fact too scared to fall in love with the wrong man? All these questions running in my head make me seem crazy. I wake up and just think where is he? When will I have a man beside me who loves me for who I am? Why do I feel so lonely? Because I do love myself, but I just want someone who loves me for ME. When will men stop trying to hurt me and start to just listen to my heart. It's as though being honest backfires on you like flames that are so hot they could leave scars on your body. Why do I confuse being drunk with being in love? You know that feeling, when you see someone when you're drunk and you just fall head over heels. Then you see them again and you don't feel the attraction but you feel that empty "love" which is actually the "need" for someone to love me. It's the desperation of the love I have never had. I crave it so much I could eat all men on this earth and find none of them are my taste but they just give me that satisfaction I need at the time. That feeling of someone gripping your hand so tightly they would never let go, that feeling of someone giving you a hug where you are so comfortable you fall asleep, that kiss that you confuse with love when it's only attraction. I think before I even fall in love I need to understand the definition of 'love'. Love isn't a one night stand or when a man gives you his undying attention until he gets what he wants and then he never speak to you again. Love is when a man is devoted to only YOU and would never look at another woman the same way. When a man opens his heart to you, you know he is here to stay. I need to be less naïve and more sincere. Understand that men aren't perfect and neither are women, but women follow their hearts & men follow their sexual drive and satisfaction. Love everything about you and the universe will love you back.

All my love,
Claire Bear. x

Stupendous contradiction.

I love you and that is all. There is nothing I can do about it. I cannot change that, even if I tried because I wish I didn't love you.

I hate that I love you and everybody hates you, some people want to kill you.... especially my cousins. They tell me you're a demonic devil but I love you, the demonic devil.

They are not wrong though are they, what a mess. Stupendous contradiction, just fucked up! People look at me like I'm crazy, they don't know, and those that do know, they don't understand.

It makes everyone sick and disgusted, it's repulsive, your repulsive, I feel sick too I want to vomit. I am sad, unwell, and I cry every day.

Rape. Raped me of my life! Raped me and my sister's for six years. You ruined our childhoods, non-existent but existence itself. I had to think hard about this its dark but the reality is I would not be writing this if you never existed. If you never existed then I would not have ever existed. I would not be alive.

I owe you my love and gratitude until the day I no longer exist. You could murder and I would forgive you. You can't reverse it you can't erase it. Life changes, my life will never be like, other girls. Some things will never change this infection in my brain, life may seem, lame but I, I do, I have existence.

Thank you for life and showing me who to trust, forgiveness to release the pain, the poison, the destruction, the devastation, breaking the cycle. To have compassion, and to love again. Not letting the past affect the future, the future may seem bleak but I shall raise my voice a little so I can release, so I can speak so I can be heard. Thank you for letting me breathe, and providing eyes to see, skin to touch. Thank you for it all, my paedophile father.

See you soon, your daughter Victoria.

But he is there.

Dear Nobody,

I hear your wailing every night. My heart senses your pain. My brain stores your memories. I have lived through your agonies. My old friend Loneliness never leaves you alone. The triplets Brutality, Contempt and Insignificance visit you too often. Trust has long ago abandoned you. She has gone to the place where Roots now resides. Hug has never shown her face. Love has never introduced herself. Unworthiness wants to take you out for the day. Low Esteem always wants to party. Empty birthdays of the past fill you. Christmas has always mocked you. Your brother, Rage, now sleeps with you. But I'm coming back, Nobody. So hold on to Hope. I know he's tiny and fragile. I know he's sick. I know you cannot see him in the dark - you have to concentrate hard to hear his voice. But he is there. Nurture him, nurse him. One day he might grow big.

Yes, I'm coming back for you, Nobody. It's been a long road full of wrong signs and deep holes - the odd mountain too. And I have been blind and one-eyed for so long. For many years I didn't want to accept you. I tried to deny you. But you lived in my head. I don't know how you got in. But you did. Yes you did, you and Hope. Most of the time you were both asleep, recovering from the wounds Trauma inflicted upon you. But then you both woke. I pretended I didn't hear you. I tried to wish you away. I broke down when you and Hope were both screaming at me. I was exhausted, spent. You and Hope too. But I remember your words before the fall.

*Motherless children,*
*If no one loves you in this world,*
*Make a start and love yourself.*

Yes, I'm coming for you, Nobody. And when I finally bless my eyes on you. I'll rename you. Yes, you're going to be somebody.

Yours sincerely
Your older self

By
*Alex 'brixtonbard' Wheatle*

Infinite.

Dear Self,

I am writing you a letter of validation and affirmation.

I rarely find the time or courage to tell you how powerful and brilliantly made you are. After all you are the identical reflection of God's unconditional love.

Self, there's a few things you should know.

- I love and accept you for who you are.
- You rest in a healthy body, your mind is brilliant and your soul is peaceful.
- You can do all things in love.
- You understand that everything that is happening now is happening for your ultimate wellbeing.
- You have the courage to say no to things that compromise your joy.
- You are the official architect of your life and you choose the content of its foundation.
- You are a forgiver of those who have harmed you consciously or unconsciously.
- You peacefully detach from those who don't mean you any good.
- You can achieve your definition of greatness.
- You are not a slave to your old habits instead you take up new and positive ones.
- You are limitless and your potential to succeed is infinite.
- You set boundaries with others to insure your soul remains at peace.
- You overflow with infinite wisdom.

You no longer have to wait for anyone else to say these words to you. You are validated.

Love,
Stephen

*-Stephen Graddick IV*

I hope you know that
kind of love too.

Dear Nadège,

I hope to share with you a few words of love and a little lesson I received in love. Actually, it's a big lesson that as a woman is often overlooked these days. I have learned only recently that self-love is invaluable. It's essential to not only our well-being but also living a fulfilled and happier life. Building self-love fosters self-esteem, enhances our life and the quality of life of the ones we care about. Sometimes the most logical thing is the hardest thing to execute. A person's life will always be fraught with stress, challenges and hurdles but if you truly love and value yourself, we are then equipped with a mental and emotional armor against those things; the energy to tackle challenges with clearer insight and perspective.

My lesson came in the form of a challenge. That challenge came with a name. Cancer. Years of self-neglect, unhappiness, discontent, fear and putting the needs of others above my own proved to be a great recipe for a physical disaster; the breakdown of my physical health. How could life possibly be over before I even understood what it is I enjoyed, liked or loved? Thankfully, I made it through the difficult journey of what too many people endure these days. My journey continues to take twists but the resounding lesson is self-care, self-preservation. Self-love. I am not talking about selfishness where a person only thinks of themselves but a deep connection with yourself. An understanding of what your wants, needs and desires are in any capacity. Do you know what it really means to love yourself, to be in love with yourself on a spiritual and emotional level? I am learning every day but I pray you are able to give yourself an enormous emotional hug sometimes. To look in the mirror each morning and consider what *you* want to do, not *only* what someone else wants. I sometimes wonder why must it take a life-altering event for us to realize that we are as important as the people and things we cherish. As women we grow and we're taught on a subconscious level to care for others, to nurture others, to love others as it's the noble, the brave and the right thing to do. From generation to generation we give ourselves to our families, friends, and romantic partners. We often groom ourselves for affection and attention but won't pamper ourselves just because we deserve it or it feels good. I spent many years believing I should not pay attention and take care of myself in any capacity because it was selfish. To buy something nice for myself, to think of myself first in any situation, to nourish my body with the right food, to take time to slow down and do nothing. To pat myself on the back when I did a good job. All these things seemed foreign and I felt underserving of even the most basic of things. Everything, every minor fancy felt like a luxury I couldn't afford. Then cancer happened. I got a fresh perspective on how important

I am to me. The world needs more people who love and cherish themselves. People like you and I. No matter where we are on this journey we call life. Self-love is what we need. I love myself enough now to know that I also deserve love and attention from me. I hope you know that kind of love too.


Love,
Effé

An intense rush.

On this day on this date in this moment in time

To whom it may concern

"What is Love?"

My beloved, from the moment we met an intense rush of an indescribable feeling moved throughout my body a feeling so intense…

Could it be love you ask yourself, could it be? What is love? Is it a feeling, an experience or just a word?

You believe you are in love confused by the images depicted on TV on posters and by those around us. Have you ever asked yourself what is love? Many confuse lust a strong sexual desire based on a physical attraction to ones appearance and fantasies of the mind and say "I love you".

Is love a feeling, an experience or just a word, its meaning many do not understand? Can you fall in and out of love or should love be forever? Do your actions determine your love for another? Ask yourself, what is love? Be true to yourself, your feelings and your actions.

On that special day of marriage,

"will you love her, comfort her, honour and protect her, and forsaking all others, be faithful to her as long as you both shall live?..."I will"

For many, love is not forever. Was it really love?

Love for me is a unification of mind, body and spiritual soul and only when all three come together will you feel an intense heat within your heart a feeling only you, your beloved one and God will know.

Love is a gift from God. Only when minds are truly willing, will your heart be filled with love.
From your love
iLoveU

Ears
hardened,
pace,
fastened.

Forget the things you thought you knew about love. The boundaries and detours you set in place to deny access to the most paradoxically inclined organ that we know of as a heart. Fragile yet resilient. Every pump a significant keeper of rhythm, and its march? Oh so militant.

I deny my heart the chance of ailment, an overprotective mother complex of sorts, prevention better than cure, a hard ears will feel moment. My ears, hardened, pace, fastened, almost too fast if I slip... at this speed... I'll die before I've mastered, cry before the laughter. So let me take my time with love for fear has made me bargain. The bounty put up on release was more than I'd imagine, resistant in my stature of course I thought I'd never allow it to happen. Consensual this was not, flowers bloomed from cement bar warning, I was always too busy trying to climb to the top that I never paid attention to falling.

Slipped my mind... tripping, momentarily lost my sight. it's different, when want & need combine.. and internal desires reign & and tame the beast that sleeps inside the deepest recesses love can find like a Determined postman searching for an address as invisible as 9 & 3 quarters.

4494

Hard.

Love is hard to define because it means different things to different people.

*-Sokario*

There is no safe way to
love someone.

# The paradox of Love

Love challenges our self-respect, by always threatening to turn joy into humiliation. Vulnerability reigns! We may scorn the incurable romantics with their hearts on their sleeves, with their heads ever ready to flip over their heels, because helpless wallowing is degrading. But we can admire the same instincts if they inspire the grand passion of truly great lovers. Vulnerability from those who lack self-respect is pitiable; when it comes from Mr Darcy it is the height of charm. We distrust love at first sight because it *feels* no different from infatuation. We only can say what it *really* was in retrospect. We use words like 'lust' or 'infatuation' in most cases when either our love is unrequited or when we lose interest; we call it 'love at first sight' when the relationship progresses and continues to grow. Whenever we fall in love, we 'take the plunge'. So to believe in love at first sight is just to believe in love – one is a subset of the other. In either case we commit to an image of our lover, and our future, which is uncertain and risks serious disappointment or pain. Love can look like a gamble. It may be that loving at first sight is a more reckless gamble than most, but from time to time even the most reckless gamble must pay off. But the other feature of romantic love is that it is beyond our control. We are helpless in the face of our lover and powerless to refuse their charms. So the term 'gamble' is misleading since it implies that falling in love is a conscious, if unwise, decision. A romantic lover is not just a reckless gambler but an addictive one. Better to think of an alcoholic who remembers how her first drink 'felt like coming home'. Dorothy Tennov coined the word *limerance* to distinguish a particular feeling associated with being in love as somewhere between infatuation, lust and obsession. She quotes Stendahl:

The most surprising thing of all about love is the first step, the violence of the change that takes places in [the] mind.... A person in love is unremittingly and uninterruptedly occupied with the image of [the] beloved.[12]

> There is no safe way to love someone - without taking a risk we are not in love. *You can only love someone who has the power to hurt you,* and by the same token, you can only be loved by someone you have the power to hurt. In other words we are simultaneously on the stage and in the audience – free, exposed, vulnerable actors on the stage, *and* stonily, silent judges in the audience. This is the paradoxical relationship between feeling free and feeling justified, which plays out when we experience love.

Take a deep breath. Read on.

A (Love) Letter to the Lucky Ones


Dear lucky one,


I hope this letter finds you alive – all senses and engines burnings – and well. It might find you waiting in line at the Christmas market. It might find you taking a break from sitting in the sun. It might find you doing research for a paper. It might find you in your most uncomfortable outfit, a little too full of life to start cleaning the kitchen – and a little too empty now that everyone's gone home. It might find you in the light, in the dark, in the back of his favourite café, in foreign places, in your parents' car, in between her cream-coloured pillows, before, after, in the midst of chaos – only, I hope, not too late.


This letter comes to tell you a few things I know to be true, in the naive hope that you won't mind me not always leading by example. You see, I believe that love, even the love radiating from a stranger's writings, is better than no love at all, and this is my way of passing it on. Love, as you know, is the only mechanism there is that can put both your warmth and your strength into motion, make you both gentler and more self-assured, sing you to sleep and ready you for war in the same voice. I will spare you the kind of love that social networks, extended families and old lovers are for – that yes, you are beautiful, unique, cared for and always welcomed home (wherever, whomever or whatever your home is) and no, not everybody can love you the same despite this. Instead I've got others, wrapped in just as much love – I promise you that. Take a deep breath. Read on.


Allow yourself to roll life between your fingers and laugh at its nonsense from time to time. You can't change overnight – we build ourselves up too strong to slip into another skin at the snap of one's fingers, even if they happen to be our own. If you truly want to become an artist, give up everything else and work on your dream for a year. If you don't achieve anything then you belong right back where you started. Nobody shows up at your door at three in the morning only to tell you that they don't love you anymore. If they do, know that they're lying. People are very bad actors. They never live up to your expectations. Let the world move at its own pace and you move at yours. Eventually there will be some collisions and some of them you'll love, but you'll never, ever love anything more than letting yourself shine through the bullshit. Never fill yourself up to the top. Let there always be room for more. Take only what is necessary. Take only what you love. *Experiences stay in you, you move out of them.* The sweetness and danger of losing control are grossly underestimated. There's a certain beauty about being a mess too, about painting outside the lines, about outstretching your arms for things at top volume, at their most difficult, at their most needlessly complex. Don't talk about fear in third person. Fear doesn't have an identity. You are the fear. Always have a world of your own. Don't be too eager to make room into someone else's. One's inner world is built on grounds that you'll never fully understand, and you'll always be cold and starved in it. Would you be happy, sleeping on the couch night after night? Complete vulnerability isn't strength. It's you losing to yourself, to your dragon, to your inner goddess. To life. Being yourself isn't about being your weakest self. Safety is not always a friend. Safety believes that life exists all around you only to be contemplated in silence. Do not enjoy touch or use it, or anxiety will grow on you like bacteria. Indulge into knowing that you've made it so far, that you're sorted, that you got to Heaven. That you are as good as dead. New-found energy is not exhausting. Still waiting is. When you're on the run, intensity felt light. You remember indecisiveness as a long stormy night, and it's just not poetic anymore. *People and their traumas don't go together like milk and cereal. If they make you their secret hiding place and you pull the curtains and let the sun in they'll leave. Not everybody wants your helping hand. Some just want your shoulder. None of your tricks can free them, because freedom isn't given, it's taken.* You can learn so much from your most badass version. Sad people are like blood clots, waiting there to kill you. Don't let them melt into you and mix it with your own. The things that you've filled up with feelings will always incline the balance in their favor. Allow the new to show you a few tricks before you reject it. Put your heart into it, but don't forget to take it back at the end of the day. Your fire is the most precious thing you'll ever have. Don't give it away.

Nobody needs it. Don't stain people with imagination and fill all the gaps with cotton candy. Let who they are shine through. Sometimes you're overly excited at the possibility of having found someone beautiful, that you risk making up miles of them. Don't. Also, don't be a vampire. Don't suck on beauty, on youth, on love; on life. Make silhouettes of spilled ink out of them and pass them on. It's the essential endurance strategy for surviving the empty soul wilderness, for all I know.

Whoever you happen to be, dear lucky one, know that I mean everything even if I don't live it all out loud. Ah, I almost forgot! One last quick piece of advice for you: always strive to make your own luck. You won't get much luckier than that.

Love, Anca (www.ancadunavete.com)

Why does it hurt you
more than it hurts me
when I'm hurt?

Never see me go without.... Even if it means you do!
Never gave up on me, when you had every right too
I could never understand why you did what you do
Why my life is more important than yours to you!
Why would you give me your last, when you're hungry as well?
Why is it so important to you that I do good in world?
Why is it so important to you that I iron my shirt?
Why does it hurt you more than it hurts me when I'm hurt?
Why have I got new shoes, when yours have holes?
Why you buy me new shit but never get yourself clothes?
Why you put your life on hold just to see me grow?
Why do you always hide your pain, thinking I don't know?
Why you still call me your baby even though I'm a man?
And you know I'm a man but won't take my helping hand!
Why why why, I don't understand.
I guess only the most high knows... it's a part of the most highs plan,
I guess it's more important I eat than you do.
I guess no matter what the world says, I'm perfect to you
I guess I ain't meant to figure out why you do what you
I just gotta know that I mean everything to you!
I must be your joy and pride
So I gotta be correct, whenever I step outside.
Your young king's everything the only wish you have in this life is to see
him win
And no matter what you're going through he can't know a thing!

You are meant to be here.

You may not know me but I knitted you together in your mother's womb, you are fearfully and wonderfully made
Psalms 139:13-14
I know when you are happy or sad
Psalms 139: 2
I know the number of hairs that are upon your head
Matthew 10:29-31
You are meant to be here, you are not an accident
Psalms 139: 15-16
I am not angry with you, neither am I far from you. I love you just as I loved my son Jesus, this is why I sent my son to gain your love
John 3:16
His ultimate sacrifice is evidence of the love I have for you
1 John 4:10
There is nothing that can separate you from my love
Romans 8:38-39
Will you accept my love? Are you willing to stop running away from me and run to me. My arms are open wide ready to accept you; Yes you. Will you be my child?
I write this letter of love to express how I feel about you and there is no doubt in my mind that I love you; no matter who you are or where you have been. My love stretches as far as the sky, as deep as the ocean and more than the multitude of stars in the night sky.
I am waiting on you.
Love from your Dad
The Almighty God

You can feel my pain.

18.11.15

You
I did not think we would be close.
We are completely different people, but we have always had unconditional love for each other.
As time went by, as I began to understand more about the ways of true love, I learnt to appreciate the things you do for me and the respect you show for my emotions. Your love speaks for itself – without words. You respect my plans, my dreams, and my passions. You can feel my pain, my anger, and my frustrations. Sometimes you can make things better. I gradually started to love you more as a person and now you have become a part of me.
Now, when I think of people who make me happy, you are in my thoughts. I have learnt a lot from you because of our differences, but the most important thing I have learnt is that you would put me before yourself and I…. would so the same for you…
Me, XX

Love is action.

Love is pain
Love is pleasure
Love is an unlimited force that can't be measured

Love is darkness
But also light
Love constrains your vision but gives you sight

Love is a vulnerability
Meant only for the strong
Who choose to dwell on the positives of people
And forgive their wrongs

Love is action
Not merely a word
But an unmerited disposition
Not won or deserved

Love is war
Love is peace
Love consoles but causes grief

Love is potent
Love is free
Love unshackles the world
But enslaves me

Love chooses its victims
What a cross to bear
When you love and hate at the same time
And the one that frees you is your snare
But love is needed
Fear not its grip
Because without love or being loved
No one has truly lived.

*-Daniel Fraser - Odin*

Blossoming.

It's been two years now, who knew we'd be where we are today; from the time we first met, to rekindling the short lived friendship we first had and it blossoming into a loving relationship. It's not been all rosy though, there have been many ups and downs but we have conquered our battles and persevered through the tough times. I have learnt so much about myself throughout the time we've been together but also how to maintain a relationship with you. Hearing about my flaws hasn't always been an easy pill to swallow but I continue to take note and do the best that I can to improve and evolve with thanks to you. We're in a beautiful place in our relationship now, which I am so grateful for, I've been longing for the days when we can laugh like we've never laughed before, joke around like we are the biggest children and spend quality time together like it is the last. I am so happy to be with you, I hope you are too and I pray that

what we have will last forever and more...with love, Chez ❤

I will always love.

I love you.

But I'm scared.

Scared of how powerful my love can be.

Sometimes I wonder.

I wonder if everyone would love like me.

I stare into my own eyes far for a moment

Followed by a laugh

I blink once.  I'm back again

Loving you is like a puzzle

So many pieces lost

But I trust my instincts

Even if my mind is misguided.

I will always love

You.

*-Auzelina Cookie*

There is no better feeling.

When I think of the word love I feel a number of emotions, both positive and negative. This has been a result of personal life experiences and relationships. For me there is no better feeling than falling 'in love' and no worse feeling that being left with a broken heart. I have experienced love at its finest and also at its worst. I have had both ups and down but within that I have learnt valuable lessons.

I have said both 'I love you' and 'I wish I never loved you'. However I have lived with no regrets through the happiness and hurt. I feel at this stage in life I am continuing to embrace love and still have faith in both the meaning and actions of love. I recognize that love might mean different things to different people but ultimately that feeling of falling remains the same for all and that is something we have no control over.

I have said many times I wish I could switch my feelings off and at times I wish I still could but I guess that would make me not human and emotions are a part of being alive! Therefore with every day I breathe I will be open to love and what that brings. Accepting that love doesn't always work out but have faith that there is still hope.

Her love still remains.

## Unconditional

Love is all about giving
Like water to a flower, love is needed for us to flourish
Love is transparent, true feelings never hidden
In its true form we're never left malnourished

Going back to where it all began
Growing up I experienced a mother's love
The kind that makes you strive to be a better son
She made me believe I could achieve anything I dreamed of

She taught me love was limitless
She taught me love was infinite
And real love was unconditional
In a world filled with violence and wickedness

Her love made me who I am today
A person of reason, forgiveness and patience
And even though her presence is no more physical
Her love still remains, only now spiritual
With Love

*-Andy Akowuah*

I dreamt my real.

## Dreaming My Real

In my head I paint images of someone, that someone is a dream.
An idea I formed from the goodness of my heart and the intelligence of my mind.
I rush my days to fall into a deep slumber to return to my cerebral craft.
Just to combine various aspects of each idea, the physical, psychology and biological.
A female I desired her to be, skin like mine?
That's okay with me.
Her physique like cola, addictive figure. Additional size in her assets may look modified but it is natural it can be.
She smiles with grace, cute angelic shaped eyes it must be a pretty face.
I made her into a compact anatomy.
Not too small but tall enough.
I still dream of the girl, I hope to meet. Forming ideas from her head to her feet.
Her heart is gold, her will can never be old, truth be told, I wonder is there more to unfold.
But one day I woke up continued my day and later on I seen my dream across the room.
I was scared that my dream would fade away like a daydreaming imagination.
Fortunately, she was very real, but she was my real.
From the moment I realised that she was present, all I wanted to do is tell her how much I love her.
Yet so frightened of not being able to dream like this again.
The thought of crushing this dreams core, the following dream wouldn't be the same.
Myself holding this love was real to me, literally feeling in my soul.
I asked myself would I ever see her or even love her again, even if it just was for one more second.
I will never know until that time comes.
At least I have someone that I care about, someone I can think about.
She was… is my love to dream about, I say this because I dreamt my real.

*-Dreya Valentino*

Agápe, Eros, Philía, and Storgē.

A Christian Letter of Love

When I think of the word love, I think Greek! Yes the Greek word for love. The Greek language is so rich. One word can envelope into a number of meanings, therefore my letter of love will describe the Greek definition of love and my Christian views on why love is an important quality to possess.

**Ancient Greek** has four distinct words for **love**: *Agápe, Eros, Philía,* and *Storgē.*

**Agápe** means brotherly love, the love of God for man and of man for God. *Agape* is used in ancient texts to denote feelings for one's children and the feelings for a spouse. Agape is used by Christians to express the unconditional love of God for mankind. Agape is selfless and sacrificial, in that it voluntarily suffers inconvenience, discomfort, and even death for the benefit of another without expecting anything in return. It is the highest of the four types of love in **the Bible**.

**Philia** is often translated as brotherly love. According to Aristotle's best-known work on ethics, **Nicomachean Ethics**, *philia* is expressed as loyalty to friends, family, and community, and requires virtue, equality, and familiarity. Furthermore, in the same text *philos* denotes a general type of love, used for love between family, between friends, a desire or enjoyment of an activity, as well as between lovers. Best friends will display this generous and affectionate love for each other as each seeks to make the other happy.

**Storge** also called familial love is the **Greek** word for natural affection such as the love of a parent towards offspring, and vice versa. It is often said that storgic lovers are friends first, and the friendship, can endure even beyond the breakup of the sexual relationship. They want their significant others to also be their best friends, and will choose their mates based on similar goals and interests.

**Éros** means love, mostly of the sexual passion. The Modern Greek word "*erotas*" means intimate love. The Bible devotes one whole book to the blessings of erotic, or sexual, love - **Song of Solomon**. However, according to that bible book, a long-term relationship based solely on *eros* is doomed to failure. The "thrill" of sexual love wears off quickly unless there are some *philia* and *agapé* to go along with it.

As a Christian, showing and displaying love is the cornerstone, without love for your fellow man you cannot be a true worshipper of God. My Heavenly father, Jehovah God is the ultimate definition of love, as he created all things for mankind, trough love in order for the family to live forever on a paradise earth which was his original purpose for mankind. The Bible gives the most beautiful definition of love, it can be found at 1 Corinthians 13:4-8.

Love is patient and kind. Love is not jealous. It does not brag, does not get puffed up, does not behave indecently, does not look for its own interests, and does not become provoked. It does not keep account of the injury. It does not rejoice over unrighteousness, but rejoices with the truth. It bears all things believes all things, hopes all things, endures all things. Love never fails.

Everything.

My Everything,

Hey beautiful, I love you and I love it when you smile, I want the whole world to know how much you mean to me. It's been love at first sight since you entered my life, I've been flying on cloud 9 and I have not come down yet.

I tell you this every day, but you are the most beautiful person I know, inside and out and I see that more clearly with each passing day. I love everything about you, about us. You do something to me that no other has, you have made me so happy, and the happiest I've ever been. You give me the most amazing feelings inside, the feeling of being in love with you.

I still don't know what I did to be so lucky to have you in my life, my dream come true... I am so thankful though. In this short time that we've been together, we have grown so much and I can't wait to see what the future holds for us. I love you always with all my heart and soul, always and forever, my Everything!!!

-*Emmanuel Adebayo*

To keep you warm.

**To you my sweetheart,**
Well how do I start? You make the hairs on the back of neck stand up, the way you smile and make me happy, I don't ever want that feeling to go. Your beautiful soft hair along with your dimples just makes me know I am extremely blessed that you're in my life. Even when we argue I still love you because that's what unconditional love is right? I love making love to you in the middle of the night and showing you a good time to show you how much I appreciate the way you treat me like a king, which enables me to treat you like a queen and appreciate every part of your beautiful body with you lying in my arms once we are done. If you're cold in the night I will make sure you have love and protection and wrap my arms around your body to keep your warm, you know why? Because you're my baby and I adore you.

I don't want this feeling to ever stop, I have never felt this way before and I know this sounds cliché, but I'm deadly serious, I would never hesitate to run you a bath if you're coming home late from work, or cook you breakfast whilst in bed, simply because you're the love of my life and I want you to understand nobody, and no one can or will ever come between that my queen. My queen I hope you can one day find it in your heart to forgive me for hurting and upsetting you, all I want to do is look after you and our beautiful children whilst providing safety and ensuring we have an amazing future, because the truth is, without you there is no me baby girl so please understand you're my everything and understand I am truly sorry babes. For richer, for poorer, till death do us part.

Yours truly,
your husband Reiss.xxxx


*-Reiss Taylor*

You stuck around when I was down without a pot to piss in.

You got some bad news... So it means I got some too!
We ain't blood brothers, but blood... it's love we're related through.
Plus your pain run through my veins, so I guess that'll do!
There's many that you'd kill for that won't ever bleed for you
That true... but with you, you've proven that's far from the truth
We're built on a foundation of love and loyalty is the roof.
We made an unspoken pact, til' death we do!
And God forbid, but if I die, my youts' are your youts' too!
And you know that it's same
If it goes da other way
And with that comforting my mind, I'mma handle your problem on my
own today,
And there's nothing you can say to make me do anything other,
These are just sacrifices that you make for your brother!

Love will make you jump in the car... knowing from this nothing good
can happen
But they put your life at risk bro...
So fuck it!
Whatever happens now just has to happen!
It is what it is,
That's how far we've come from and where we've been.
Remembering when we had nothing... But still shared everything!
Remember when you stuck around when I was down without a pot to piss
in?
Certain people disappeared when the money did but you were never
missing.
It's these little memories why I will give you everything!
Why I drop everything if that phone ever decides to ring
In a world where most speak behind your back.... you ride when I ain't
even there.
So this can never be a favour, it's repayment yeah,
In debt to each other for the rest of our years
But this is far from a burden it's a pleasure you hear!
Whether I'm wrong or right you ride right by my side
You'll walk into the fire for your brudda knowing its suicide!
And that the same reason why you didn't get a call
Cos if it all goes wrong at least I'm the only one to fall!
So as I prepare to risk all... one up in my bally and gloves.
I hold warmth in my heart knowing love is love!

A golden glow of light.

To my children, my love, my life.

My fantastic children, there are days when you may think I don't like being your mum. When you look at me and I am scowling and cross, I am ranting and shouting. I am shattered at the end of the day; I have cleaned, washed all the washing, been to work and cooked your tea. You all want my attention; I am frustrated as you repeat the same question over and over, each sentence starting with 'MUM'. I sometimes think can I take anymore, I want to shout just give me some space!

But then I stand and look, reflect, and remember how, I held your tiny little hands and I have seen them grow, I have seen your confidence and character develop, you are the little people who have had me on my knees playing.

I have learnt that there are little people who are more important to me; you have taught me what patience is, how to be compassionate and more understanding, and what the value of life really is.

I have waited on you, sat up all night worried when you were ill, I have stood by the door waiting on your first time out alone, I cried when I left you for the first time at nursery. You have left me mentally and physically exhausted, but you are the best thing, and most precious thing in my life, I am proud to say you are 'MY beautiful children'

You have no idea now, of how precious you are, how I look and just see a golden glow of light beaming from you, you smile and I feel warm inside, we hug and I feel alive.

This love is unconditional; I can forgive my new makeup being thrown down the toilet, finding my best silk shoes being worn in the wet garden, and all the heads of my prized flower garden being presented to me with a huge smile.

This love is reciprocal; we hug with love, we hug for comfort, we hug because we can. We kiss good morning, we kiss goodbye and hello, we kiss because we can. We look into each other's eyes and we know the true unconditional love and bond of a mother and child that will never be broken.

These are my children; they are my love and my life, now and forever.

-*Sharron Stevens-Smith*

Love is the strongest painkiller.

Love, that special feeling that makes you smile.
Yes! It takes you to cloud nine or even higher.
You feel like you can touch the stars.
Loving and being loved fills your soul with bliss,
Giving you keys to unlock chambers of joy and peace.
Love is a priceless gift.

Love brings sunshine into your life.
Love is like a shield, it protects, like a blanket,
It gives warmth and like booze, it gets you intoxicated.
Life is full of heartaches and pains but love is the strongest painkiller,
It squashes pain.

If the world had love, we would have paradise on earth.
Five a day plus love is all we need to be healthy and happy.
Love is the most essential nutrient for the human soul.

*-Sam Akande*

Love is just as potent
as hate.

Love is just as potent as hate
Hate is just as potent as love,
They both spread like wildfire with a burning passion.
To give your love to someone you love is dangerous and leaves you
vulnerable as they are free to do what they want with it and if you are
unfortunate to have your love abused,
You might end up stuck in the vibration of hate wondering how you got
there when it all stemmed from love.
What I thought love was as a child is somewhat different to the "love" I
have been in and experienced,
Which is completely different to what I feel love is now.
It must be whatever you feel it to be at the time.
So how can I really define love?
It must be a combination of a past, present and future thought
Mama earth is a manifestation of universal love
but we as a people on this earth love to hate,
love to destroy and love to love.

So it must be anything and everything.

*-Belevia.D.Neturu*

There will be more love.

**HERE** we are love it's Monday and the edges of the sky look a bit dark. Nothing has turned out how you thought it would. Every plan you've ever made dissolved, effervesced between your fingers. When you got what you asked for the edges were sharper and the corners were harder than you were prepared for. So far there have been tears and blood, scrapes, broken bones and tattered hearts. The roads have been labyrinthine, borderline unfathomable and more times than not you found your compass inverted, caught on the wrong end of north. You've seen the dark days, the cloudy days. Days heavy with so much water you felt like you were drowning a hundred miles from sea.

When it bothered, the world taught you many things, painful things. Among them it taught you how to hate, how to be afraid and sadly, it taught you how to hide the soft corners of your heart behind an ivory cage. If asked you would never admit that alongside with the acid taste of fear and the familiar shiver of dread crawling along your skin you learned something else, how to love. Yes, the world was often darker than you wanted it to be and the aching repetition of failure has been a more constant teacher than anything or anyone else ever was.

All these are truths, and they will remain truths. There will be failures and heartaches and losses in the time to come. Don't despair because more importantly, there will also be more love. I can't promise the best outcome or that you'll always do right, half the time you won't. What matters is the half that you get it right. Let those moments of delirious, incandescent joy, fuel the mechanics of your heart. Let that joy light the darkness that is yet to come.

All my love,

N.L. Shompole.

# Acknowledgements

I would like to thank my aunts for showing me how it looks to overcome an inconceivable amount of struggle and providing me the foundation and the tools that I use every day. Thank you for seeing what I do not see, much of who I am today is because of your work and I am so grateful to you for that.

I would like to thank my friends for holding my hand through it all; I always know that I am loved with you. I would like to thank the leaving care team at the University of Greenwich for supporting me over the past four years, and The Big House Theatre Company for providing me a platform to move and connect with others. I would like to thank Mwila, Dubem, Reanne and Trent for sticking with me and holding me down through this course.

Thank you Sarah for having the audacity to set-up an organization as revolutionary as the What If Academy and for showing me a commitment to young people and for a better world that I have never, ever seen in my life.

Thank you to all 46 authors for sending such beautiful Letters of Love. Thank you for seeing value in the vision and for having the commitment and generosity to get behind it, having people like you in the world makes it so much better.

Thank you,
Michael Gichia
Rio Hamilton

Sam Akande

Jennifer Q

Sharron Stevens–Smith

Tox Mahogany

Andy West

Effé Laurent

Shannen L. Gilbert

Robin Clisby

Janice René

Anca Dunavete

Mona Nelson

Wendy Adams-Rickerby

Andy Akowuah

Jason Morgan

Bobbi Byrne

Dreya Valentino

LionHeart

N.L. Shompole

Chezelle Hussey

Belevia.D.Neturu

Reiss Taylor

Auzelina Cookie

Daniel Fraser-Odin

Stephen Graddick IV

Alex 'brixtonbard' Wheatle

Lisa Samuels

Natalie Berry

Jemal 'Big J' Peters

Fabian Jones

Emmanuel Adebayor

Nadège x